STAMMERER'S TONGUE

STAMMERER'S TONGUE

by

DAVID HEAD

A book of prayers for the infant Christian

New York
THE MACMILLAN COMPANY
1960

For Martin John,
whose infant tongue will
soon be speaking plainly

PREFACE

This book is a sequel to *He Sent Leanness*. At that statement, some readers may immediately remember a previous engagement, and hurry away. It cannot be helped. Truth will out, and facts are stubborn as mules.

That first little book contained prayers for the "natural man," who is the "old man" in all of us. It set out to show how the natural man prays, and attempted to put into words the kind of things he actually wants. (You did not come across it? You may yet find a copy in the British Museum if you hurry.)

This book follows the same pattern, but between the two publications the natural man has got converted. It does happen! He is now learning how to pray and what to pray. If he ever reads a book, he will find plenty to help him with his prayers. (See the Notes.) This book, at most, can only show him how he prays now in his Christian infancy, and give him the faintest glimmer of what may come later. It is written to egg on, not to warn off, the stammerer. If the most aweful thing about prayer is that God hears it, the most wonderful thing about prayer is that God wants to listen to it.

The mature Christian, so much needed in this adolescent age, will purchase his meat elsewhere. Here is but liquid nourishment—and we hope refreshment.

I am very grateful to the Reverend Dr. J. Alan Kay for his encouragement and detailed suggestions. The

Questions and Notes at the end are intended to increase the usefulness of the book, for those who will take the trouble. There is a Postback, as before. We are asked, Why not call it an Appendix? But that really would be tempting the publishers. Appendices exist to be taken out.

Radcliffe-on-Trent, Nottingham

CONTENTS

Contents

PROLOGUE

But what am I?
An infant crying in the night:
An infant crying for the light:
And with no language but a cry.

ALFRED LORD TENNYSON

What are our lame praises in comparison of His love?
Nothing, and less than nothing; but love will stammer
rather than be dumb.

ARCHBISHOP LEIGHTON

Thou, Jesu, Thou my breast inspire,
And touch my lips with hallowed fire,
And loose a stammering infant's tongue.

CHARLES WESLEY

INQUIRE OF THE LORD

She went to inquire of the Lord.

In that day ye shall ask me nothing. Verily, verily, I say unto you, Whatsoever ye shall ask the Father in my name, he will give it you.

Hitherto have ye asked nothing in my name: ask, and ye shall receive, that your joy may be full.

These things have I spoken unto you in proverbs: but the time cometh, when I shall no more speak unto you in proverbs, but I shall show you plainly of the Father.

At that day ye shall ask in my name.

I

Under correction

(a) on the circumference

one of the company
> Master, speak to my brother, that he divide the inheritance with me.

the Jews
> What shall we do, that we might work the works of God?

a father

If thou canst do any thing, have compassion on us, and help us.

a Samaritan woman

From whence then hast thou that living water? Art thou greater than our father Jacob?

Nicodemus

How can a man be born when he is old?

the disciples of John

Art thou he that should come, or do we look for another?

one of His disciples

Lord, suffer me first to go and bury my father.

(*b*) *the inner circle*

From whence can a man satisfy these men with bread here in the wilderness?

Master, who did sin, this man, or his parents, that he was born blind?

Lord, Increase our faith.

Tell us, when shall these things be?

Lord, wilt thou at this time restore again the kingdom to Israel?

(*c*) *Peter*

Depart from me.

Let us make here three tabernacles; one for thee, and
one for Moses, and one for Elias.

How oft shall my brother sin against me, and I forgive him? till seven times?

Although all shall be offended, yet will not I.

Lord, I am ready to go with thee, both into prison
and to death.

Lord, why cannot I follow thee now? I will lay down
my life for thy sake.

Lord, and what shall this man do?

(*d*) the others

Martha

Lord, dost thou not care that my sister hath left me
to serve alone? bid her therefore that she help me.

Andrew

There is a lad here, which hath five barley loaves, and
two small fishes: but what are they among so many?

Thomas

Lord, we know not whither thou goest, and how can
we know the way?

Philip

Lord, shew us the Father, and it sufficeth us.

2

For all occasions

(*a*) Advent

Lord, I am not sure what this Second Coming is all

about, and it sounds a bit terrifying; but as long as it is You who are coming, I don't mind.

(*b*) *Bible Sunday*

Don't let the preacher tell me again that I ought to read my Bible. I need, not an "ought" but a "how." At present it is "read, mark, learn, and inward indigestion."

(*c*) *Christmas*

Christmas has come and gone, and this year as usual there has hardly been a minute to meditate on the Incarnation. Please help me to do better at Easter, in spite of the fact that we shall have a houseful of visitors.

(*d*) *Covenant Sunday*

How can I pray, "Let me have nothing," when I want so much?

(*e*) *Epiphany*

Give us power, not only to launch a sputnik, but to follow a star.

(*f*) *Ash Wednesday*

Lord, I think perhaps I ought to be more disciplined in my TV viewing during Lent, but whatever should I do with my time?

(*g*) *Good Friday*

I know I should be thinking a lot more about Thy suffer-

4

ing, and not only on this day. But so often when I try to begin, I find all sorts of questions in my mind about the Atonement. Can it be Thy determined will that we human beings should be saved in a way we cannot fully understand? Should I be ready to accept something with the heart that I cannot grasp with the head? Help me to distinguish credulity from faith. Help me to be teachable. Perhaps I turn away from Thy Cross because not only its difficulties but its demands are so great. Help me to see and adore, to look and live.

(*h*) *Easter*

May I celebrate the Resurrection every Sunday, and experience it every day of the week.

(*i*) *Low Sunday*

How easy it is to feel "under the weather." Keep the depression over Iceland, and show me how to be a Christian with a stinking cold.

(*j*) *Ascension Day*

"Going up," "sitting," "standing," "throne," "right hand" . . . No doubt these pictures were very helpful once, and still are to some. Help me to think hard about their meaning, and not be put off by mental images belonging to a different world from the one I know.

(*k*) *Whit Sunday*

Lord, I do not know what goes on inside the nuclear

reactor, but the released energy lights my reading lamp, heats my water, and cleans my carpet. May Thy mysterious Spirit of power within bring me light, and heat, and cleansing winds.

(*l*) *Trinity Sunday*

Lord, this doctrine is too much for me, and apparently too much for this morning's preacher. The sermon was about kindness to animals.

(*m*) *Young People's Day*

May they see that Thou art not simply offering security,
  but demanding sacrifice.
May they see that Thou art not simply making demands,
  but offering life.

(*n*) *Sunday School Anniversary*

"Let saints on earth in concert sing."
These little saints their praises bring.
Save and deliver us, we pray,
From nonstop concert here today.

(*o*) *Harvest Festival*

Don't let us turn the whole thing into a parable of spiritual realities. Thou art Creator as well as Redeemer, and we do appreciate apples and bread, even if we are not very fond of squash.

6

(*p*) *Overseas Missions Anniversary*

We thank Thee for a real live missionary, and pray for a few more real live collectors.

(*q*) *Holy Communion*

I am trying truly and earnestly to repent of my sins, though I fail in so many subtle ways that I grow bewildered when I seek to think of them one by one. I hope I am in love and charity with my neighbors, though the standard of perfect love is so terribly demanding. I really do intend to lead a new life, though I am discouraged by what has happened to previous intentions. I could not dare to take this holy Sacrament to my comfort, without the amazing knowledge that Thou art inviting me to come. For that reason, and only for that reason, I draw near with faith.

(*r*) *on the hills*

Why am I so much more conscious of awe and mystery here than in Church?

(*s*) *feeling guilty*

Lord, I have told Thee all about this without much sense of relief. Is it Thy voice telling me to talk to someone else about it? Why is that so much more difficult?

(*t*) *before breakfast cereal*

O Lord, make me crisp and always ready to serve. (With affectionate acknowledgments to the Reverend Alfred Lawson, serving in the Church in Eastern Nigeria.)

(*u*) *on washday*

Save me from dullness, as well as from dirt. Add brightness to whiteness.

(*v*) *at the conveyor belt*

O God, nothing faulty slips past Your eyes. Yet You do not cast me out.

(*w*) *in the garden*

May all Thy creatures be fed, but not entirely off my lettuces.

(*x*) *at cricket*

The Lord bless my going in and my coming out.

(*y*) *in business*

From false profits,
Overtaxing and underselling,
And shares that go bump in the night,
Good Lord deliver us.

(z) *going to bed*

I'm worried about this. I'm angry with myself about that. I'm resentful against him. I'm attracted by her. I'm restless and tense. Is there a Christian way of going to bed?

3
Weather—or not

Lord, those children! Thou knowest that it is the Sunday School Outing tomorrow, and how important it is to them. If only there was more to *do* at M—— when it rains. There are not enough movies, and they all get so crowded during bad holiday weather. Apart from the sands and the sea and the arcades, there is just *nowhere* to go.

Ought I to pray for fine weather? Isn't it terribly presumptuous? Probably the farmers are praying for something quite different. Shouldn't we confine our prayers to people rather than things? Thou art the Lord of land and sea, the God who speaks in the floods and the thunder. Wilt Thou not speak also in the lack of floods? Is it not Thy sun which is as a bridegroom coming out of his chamber? Did not our Lord rule the waves and the wind? Can our prayers affect the course of nature? Elijah's prayer shut the heavens up, but perhaps he was different.

How difficult it all is! May it not be best for us humans to leave it entirely to Thee, and not to mess about?

What a muddle it would be if we could control the weather. It even looks as though we are going to. "Part of the subjection of nature to man," the Lesson Notes said last Harvest Festival. I do not suppose the scientists will take Sunday School Outings into their calculations. But Thou, Lord, art a lover of children, and the giver of happiness. If Thou wilt, and if I am not speaking out of turn, do Thou confound the official forecasters, and give us a sunny day.

4
Let your yea be yea

O Lord,
I am a man of little faith,
and I dwell in the midst of a people of little faith.
When I pray,
help me to believe that Thou dost hear,
and that Thou dost answer.
They say there are no unanswered prayers.
Help me to accept that, not only as an intellectual
proposition, but as an undoubted inner conviction.
Help me to remember it as I pray.

They say Thou dost sometimes say No, as any earthly
father must.
They say Thou dost often say Wait, but waiting in
hopeful expectancy is about the hardest thing in the
world to do. May I wait without fretting, fussing, or
flapping. May I wait without despairing.

Sometimes I think the answer is neither No, nor Wait, but rather, "That depends on the cooperation of one of My servants."

Can it possibly be true that Thy hands are tied by human indifference and inactivity?

Is it our most grievous fault that men starve and suffer in spite of our prayers?

Do I miss a blessing when others are disobedient?

Do others fail to receive Thy help when I am unwilling?

No. . . . Wait. . . . If. . . . Surely it is Yes sometimes!

Some people talk as though the answer were always Yes. I have not found it so.

Some people pray as though the answer could never possibly be Yes. That cannot be right.

What does it mean to pray the prayer of faith? Does it simply mean leaving it to Thee? St. James says the prayer of faith shall heal!

Clearly, I must not always expect Yes, when I pray for a change of circumstances.

Safe journeys, rain after sowing, four-wheeled private transport, a family of four (two boys, two girls), a larger house . . .

It must be right to share all this with Thee, but wrong to expect spoonfeeding.

Then, why didst Thou say, "Ask, and you shall receive"?

Why didst Thou say, "It shall be given you"?

What are these words, "Nothing doubting"? and "Believe that you have received them, and you shall have them"?

I think I see!

Prayers for the Kingdom, for grace, for the inward life, always receive Thy ready affirmative.

I pray for cleansing, for guidance, for filling.

All this is already promised in Christ, in whom is the Yea and Amen.

"It is always Yes with Him."

All this Thou art willing to give.

All this is knocking on the door, with Thee.

To pray is not to beg a reluctant King, but to admit a waiting One.

To pray is not to persuade, but to surrender.

So the Holy Spirit is given to those who ask— given freely, given always.

The petition in Christ's name is always granted; His stamp is upon it.

The Father knows how to give good gifts to His children.

To the prayer for holy love, the answer is always Yes.

CHURCH MILITANT

Let us pray for the whole estate of Christ's Church militant here on earth.

We humbly beseech Thee . . . to inspire continually the universal Church with the spirit of truth, unity, and concord:

And grant, that all they that do confess Thy holy Name, may agree in the truth of Thy holy word, and live in unity and godly love.

Give grace, O heavenly Father, to all the Ministers of Thy Gospel . . . and to all Thy people give Thy heavenly grace; and especially to this congregation here present.

SERVICE OF HOLY COMMUNION

5
The great congregation

(*a*) *the preacher*

May it be
   not my word aimed at my glory,
   nor Thy word aimed at my glory,
   nor my word aimed at Thy glory,
   but Thy word, through me, to Thy glory, through
     us all.

(*b*) *the restless listener*

Not for me the seat of the scornful, but why must the

seat of the righteous always be so hard and uncomfortable?

(c) the steward in the vestry
We thank Thee for Thy servant who has come among us. We know something of his gifts and reputation. There are some who have come specially this evening because his name was on the board. Grant him all the grace and wisdom he needs. And now, Lord, as we enter Thy sanctuary, blot him out.

(d) the West African visitor
Lord, why do they all seem so determined to look stiff and unhappy, and why are they ashamed to say Amen at the end of a prayer?

(e) the choirmaster
When, oh, when, will the choir *live* in harmony together?

(f) the organist
Forgive me that so often my left hand does not know what my right hand is doing, and at the end of the service may I say with the Psalmist,

"Thou hast enlarged my steps under me, that my feet did not slip."

(g) the child
The children's address seems to be giving the grownups plenty of amusement. May there be something in the sermon that I can enjoy.

14

(h) the sacramentalist
There is so little to delight the eyes and the heart. Help me get beyond the wall text and the shabbiness and the ugly organ, and to endure, as seeing the invisible. If there be no other beauty, may I recognize the beauty of holiness.

(i) the undergraduate
I am tired of clever sermons. Tell me the story simply.

(j) Old Sam, in the back pew as usual
Speak up, Lord, for Thy servant heareth with the greatest difficulty.

(k) the schoolboy, who has given up the struggle during the second prayer
34 and 428 and 168 and 46 and 386! If only we could sing "The Lord's my shepherd" instead of "I sing the almighty power," the total would give the Battle of Hastings.

(l) the would-be worshiper
Lord, I suppose I come out of habit, to see my friends, to enjoy the singing, to hear the preacher, to learn something, to get help for the coming week, to restore my sense of values, and for a hundred other reasons. But now I am here, let me worship.

(m) the reluctant sidesman
Thou knowest I have little desire to dwell in the tents

15

of wickedness, but honestly I would rather not be a doorkeeper in the house of my God.

(n) the young man in love
May she be in the choir again today, and may she sing only for me—and, of course, Thee.

(o) the lover of old favorites
So many new tunes! Help me to worship Thee, even when praise sits silent on my tongue. Forgive me that without Sankey, I'm moody.

6
Visible Church

Lord, I pray for the Church—Thy Church—that wonderful and sacred mystery, which is Thy visible Body on earth. I am perplexed by a Church that seems to draw on invisible springs for its vitality and renewal, yet cannot exist without councils, collections, and caretakers. I have been so busy with a round of Church activities. Now I feel the need to think things out again. Help me to do my thinking in Thy Presence, otherwise I am bound to go far astray.

Only in recent years has the Church as a fellowship and an organization meant much to me. Everything I was taught as a child stressed individual conversion, individual experience, and individual worship. The Christians I knew seemed to regard their coming together as a useful way of getting things done. They used to talk sometimes about the invisible Church, the members of which were known only to Thee, but it was too invisible to make much difference. A man stuck to his denomination so long as it gave him what he wanted, like my old Sunday school teacher who became a ———ist because their prayer meetings were half an hour longer. The main thing was "holiness," which meant a spiritual glow and a perpetual no, and if the people around you were not sufficiently "holy," it was best to go and look for others who were, or found your own denomination with a membership of one.

When Thou didst convert me, granting me a real experience of Thy grace, my mind was full of Thee and me, and nothing else seemed to matter. Perhaps that was right then. But I could not stay there. Now I see that the Church is part of Thy good news, the gift of Thy Spirit, Thy family on earth, and the foretaste of the family life of heaven.

But where is the visible Church? I was converted in a ———ist Church, and have been a member ever since. But I want to live as a Christian, rather than a ———ist. Is that wrong? Are we proud of our own particular denomination and its special treasures in the wrong way? Do we—perhaps often—put it before the Kingdom? I want to belong to Thy Church, Thy worshiping, witnessing, visible Church. How can I do that, except by belonging to one part of it? Which part? Can I be a loyal member of my denomination, yet think of myself as a member of Thy Church, and work for the coming great Church, which is part of Thy will for earth?

Like everyone else, I have my own beliefs about things. At present I think that believers' baptism is best, but that infant baptism can be full of meaning and importance. I believe that the Holy Spirit can be given at any time, but I do not doubt that He is given in the service of Confirmation. I think the government of the Church should be in the hands of the local congregation, but that there is a lot to be said for the Methodist circuit system. I think there should be room in our worship for "read" prayers, extempore prayers, and silence. I think we should have Holy Communion once a week, as the early Church did, and make it the central act of worship—with sermon. I believe in the laying on of hands for healing, and anointing with oil. I believe in exorcism and evangelism through revival hymns. I believe that women should be ordained to the ministry—only a few, after much care! I recognize the value of brass bands and bishops. Then where do I belong?

I believe Holy Communion is Thy gift and Thy command; yet there are great lovers of Thee in the Salvation Army. I would use the word "authority" of the Bible, but not the word "infallible"; yet Thou hast many fundamentalist friends. I am helped by dignified worship, but pentecostal handclapping is not heresy. I think the Roman Catholic Church is in grievous error, but Thou dost use it to produce saints. How can I judge where is the true Church?

Have we taken too much upon ourselves Thy prerogative of judgment? Have we insisted upon things which Thou in Thy revealed Word didst never insist upon? Have we even dared to make ultimate judgments about others? Have we confused worship with one exclusive form of ritual? Have we confused belief with certain intellectual propositions? Have we in Thy Name been hard, petty, and uncharitable? Yet Thou knowest we must follow the truth as we see it, and principles must be upheld. Thou knowest that we are both the glad inheritors and the bewildered servants of the treasures of the past. Show us where we need to be strong, and where we need to be humble. Show us Thy Church, in visible purity, in visible unity.

Where is Thy Church to be found?
Dare I believe that it is where two or three are gathered together in Thy Name?
Dare I believe that it is where one man prays, and is linked in prayer with all the members of the Body?
Dare I believe that it is here, now?

Thy Presence makes the feast.
Thy Presence makes the Church.
Thou art in the midst of us, and we are called by Thy Name.

7
A mouth and wisdom

I will give you a mouth and wisdom

LUKE 21:15

(a) His servants the prophets

O my Lord, I am not eloquent, neither heretofore, nor since thou hast spoken unto thy servant; but I am slow of speech, and of a slow tongue.

Woe is me! for I am undone; because I am a man of unclean lips, and I dwell in the midst of a people of unclean lips: for mine eyes have seen the King, the Lord of hosts.

Ah, Lord God! Behold, I cannot speak: for I am a child.

(b) the politician

Looking through my notes for this evening's public meeting, O Lord, and examining them in the light of Thy revealed truth, I am considerably shocked. So many of the ideas are other people's, presented as my own. I find I have so little real concern for some of the things I intend to get heated about. So much consists in a vigorous and rather petty tearing to pieces of the other side. I have never been one of the "absolute honesty" enthusiasts, but surely one must be comparatively honest.

For once in my life I have tried on a second reading to eliminate bombast, negative criticism, scoring party points by assuming righteous indignation, invective, and appeals to self-interest.

Lord, what is left may be without guile, but it is frightfully dull.

(c) the schoolteacher

Thou knowest the difficulties of teaching Scripture.

Even if I am sometimes ignorant, muddled, incoherent, and unintelligible, may I always be interesting, for there is nothing drab about Thy ways.

And may I have the children's genuine respect, without unknowingly assuming Thy omniscience.

(d) the radio announcer

Lord, I am tired of reading other people's praises,
Saying my prayers in other people's phrases.
I'm as tired of secondhand confession of my sins,
As I am of reading other fellows' news bulletins.
O may I pray
Extempore,
Though I'll never be allowed to give the news that way.

(e) the trade-union member

They are always emphasizing that a Christian should take an active part in trade-union meetings. Now I am here, Lord, I don't know what to say, and I am not sure that I'd have the courage to say it if I did. Can I get some help before next time—and who from?

(f) the anxious parent

It is quite time I talked to Mary about serious matters. When she was small we used to say a lot to each other about babies and God. But over the past few years we have talked together less and less, except about homework and hockey and cooking and clothes.

Am I no longer the right person to speak to her about life and its methods and its Source? Must it be left to the teacher or the minister or, much worse, to the gossip of the dance hall and the walk home? O Lord, help me to build up anew the sort of relationship which will make it possible to speak without embarrassment of the beauty of sex and the beauty of holiness.

(g) *the embryonic lay preacher*
Thou, Lord, hast given me a message, a voice, and an opportunity. My eyes are upon my notes, and occasionally on my congregation. My voice is already uplifted, and directed to the back of the church. My feet are firmly planted in the pulpit, slightly apart. But, please tell me, whatever can I do with my hands?

(h) *the new candidate for the Ministry*
O my Lord, the whole thing is quite impossible. The thought of a minister's life appals me. The thought of a minister's responsibilities terrifies me. That Thou shouldst entrust Thy word to my faltering lips, and Thy sacraments to my shaking hands!

Thou knowest the sort of man I am, how most of the time I like to keep in the background, how occasionally I like to bask in the sun of public approval. A minister is not allowed the obscure places, and it must be fatal if he shows off!

Life has always been a bit muddled. Not for me the clear guidance, the well marked line of action, the obvious course of duty and love. Yet somehow one step has followed another. Gifts and graces—they are sparse enough. What sort of fruit has my Christian life produced so far? I suspect I seldom even blossom!

How can a man be sure? No dream, no special revelation, only a thought stated by a trusted friend, a word that set a new wheel turning, and opened up a new world. So now the imagination goes haywire, and the emotions keep changing color, and the will hangs back. What is it waiting for? Somehow the thing is settled, before I decide to settle it. The door is passed, before my feet start to walk. Let the Church decide, then. If I am mistaken, may the Spirit make it clear.

As Thou hast called me to Thy service, make me worthy of my calling.

8

Praying with the Bible

"Behold, I send you forth as sheep in the midst of wolves: be ye therefore wise as serpents, and harmless as doves."

MATTHEW 10:16, using Revised Version with marginal references

You

Must I accept these words as the Lord's command to me? Jesus was speaking to the twelve apostles. What is it St. Mark says about them?—That He chose them "that they might be with Him." That was the beginning of the Church. Jesus speaks to them again and again as one group—"you." They were such different types. The only thing they had in common was the choosing of Christ.

We are a mixed bunch at my local church. Are we together, and have we to put up with each other, for the one good reason that Christ called us? We do not seem very different from the rest of the world. How are we different? We all share human nature. Are we different because our life "is hid with Christ in God"? Is that where I am?

> Lord, I thank Thee for Thy call to me, and to people like me.
> I confess the sin of the world, including my own.
> I pray for humility

Sheep

Sheep are harmless, unprotected creatures. But for Jewish listeners the word "sheep" would mean much more than that. The Old Testament is full of references to Israel as the flock of God. In Jesus the Shepherd came Himself to seek "the lost sheep of Israel" (verse 6), and the "other sheep which are not of this fold."

Jesus said that His sheep hear His voice, and follow Him. I think I am not very sensitive to His voice. I think my Christian life is too isolated. Should I start going to the weeknight Fellowship again?

> Lord, I thank Thee that Thy Church inherits all the great promises.
> I remember those in this neighborhood who are not far from Thy Kingdom and Thy fold.
> I pray for fellowship.

Send forth
"Shepherd" is a warm and tender word. Christ's sheep, as we sing sometimes, "are fed, on Thy bosom reclined, And screened from the heat of the day." In all ages, when Christians have been exposed to the bare teeth of the world, they have clearly known that security.

But do pastors and congregations sometimes put sheep pens round themselves? Are we, in the Church in this town, too full of ourselves, too wrapped up in ourselves? Jesus leads out His flock. Apostles are those who are sent. The margin refers to John 17:18: "As thou didst send me into the world, even so sent I them into the world." Is this the mark of the "apostolic Church"?

Lord, I thank Thee for Thy clear commission to go out.
I seek Thy guidance, as I help our leaders to reorder our Church life for the sake of "those outside."
I pray for courage.

Wolves
This mission of the Church is to be carried out among wolves. There is fierce, unreasonable, devouring human opposition to be faced. In some countries, it is the power-backed hostility of the State. For people like me, it means enduring the sneer and the cold shoulder and the sense of being "out" of things. For the Church or the Christian not suffering wolves, there are the dangers of lukewarmness and respectability.

For Christ, the greatest suffering was not *from* wolves,

but *for* them. It is not easy to follow Him who was led like a lamb to the slaughter. What a costly business loving people is!

> Lord, I thank Thee for all Churches under persecution, and for all Christians who maintain their love for others at great price.
> I bring to Thee all who hate Thy Church, and resist Thy truth.
> I pray for compassion.

Wise

I suppose this is the practical wisdom of the man who chooses the right ends and the best way of reaching them. People like that, committed to the values of the Gospel, look foolish to the world. They share the foolishness of God. Such a man may look foolish, but I do not think he ought to look "sheepish." His "grasp" (the old-fashioned word is "prudence") will go far beyond the wisdom of "the children of this world," because for him infinitely more is at stake—the salvation of the world.

How much do we in the Church of today show this down-to-earth wisdom? Do I bring to the strategy of proclaiming the Gospel and doing good to all men the careful planning which goes with arranging holidays or pursuing hobbies?

> Lord, I thank Thee for the wisdom that comes down from above.

Make me more efficient and more effective in bringing others to Thee, and using all opportunities for
good.
I pray for wisdom.

Harmless

The serpent is the traditional symbol for wisdom, but
also for craft and subtlety. The margin mentions Genesis
3:1, which is the story of the serpent in Eden. So Jesus
adds, "Be harmless as doves." The sheep must not be
wolfish in heart or behavior. The Revised Version gives
another translation—"simple." My Commentary says
the original word literally means "without horns." I suppose we might say "without twists."

Does this mean that we are to be wise, but not over-
subtle? How easily Christians become cynics! When
did I last pull someone else's motives to pieces, and suspect the worst? When we get hurt or overburdened, our
conversation gets an edge on it. The margin refers to
similar ideas in Philippians 2:15 and I Corinthians 14:20,
and to Romans 16:19 where Paul seems to have the
words of Jesus Himself in mind: "I would have you
wise unto that which is good, and simple [that must be
the same word] unto that which is evil."

Lord, I thank Thee for all men and communities
who defeat subtle temptations in Thy strength.
Restore all Christians who compromise themselves
unknowingly, or who lose their innocence under
the attack of wolves.

27

I pray for simplicity, and for the love that "taketh not account of evil."

Behold, I

What a lot in a small verse! The call of God's flock, their situation in the world, and the character they need, all are here. But the most important word is certainly "I," spoken by Christ of Himself. It is He who calls, He who knows the circumstances of service, He who equips His people.

I do not think I am very obedient. I do not seem to have much courage. My life is ineffective, and my thoughts are complicated. Thank God I do not have to be worthy before I can belong to the flock of Christ. His call is everything. In His great mercy He has chosen me to be with Him and with His people, and He sends us out in company to proclaim Him as the good Shepherd who gave His life for the sheep.

My Shepherd and my Lord, lead me. I pray for willingness to be led. Amen.

OUT OF THE DEPTHS

Out of the depths have I cried unto thee, O Lord.
Lord, hear my voice: let thine ears be attentive to the
voice of my supplications.
If thou, Lord, shouldest mark iniquities, O Lord, who
shall stand?
But there is forgiveness with thee, that thou mayest be
feared.
I wait for the Lord, my soul doth wait, and in his word
do I hope.

PSALM 130:1–5

9
Very dry
(*a*)

O Lord, talking to Thee is like talking to a brick wall.

(*b*)

Eternal God, I have been brought up in the Church all my life. I recognize my home for what it is—a good Christian home. I have been taught the great truths of faith, and think I know something of their meaning. I have made my earnest decision to follow Christ, and I have been received into the full membership of the Church. I worship regularly, and teach in the Sunday school.

Why is it I *feel* so little?

(c)

Lord, my work becomes increasingly demanding, the
family is requiring more attention these days, I have
taken on more offices at Church than I can possibly do
well (but there seems to be nobody else willing), my
diary is full and I can do nothing in a leisurely way,
and so many people want to tell me their troubles. I
feel tired and empty. Must love always be so costly?
And what does one do with weariness in well-doing?
And must I take a holiday from Church affairs, or can
I learn to refuel in flight?

(d)

Father, I am not sure that I have ever been conscious
of Thy Presence. But I have often been vividly conscious
of Thy absence, as I am now. Forgive my self-indul-
gence, and if I cannot yet soar in heavenly places, save
me from the heaviness of hell.

(e)

Almighty God, I came to this country with such high
hopes. My family was thrilled for me to come. My
Church gave me a great send-off. What higher privilege
than to be a student in the United Kingdom? I arrived
with excitement and expectancy.

Now, after a few months, I go around with disap-
pointment—even resentment. I seem hedged in by difficulties. I find release only with my African friends,

some of whom have said goodbye to Church and faith.

Why is it so hard for me? Is it the strenuous, ever-demanding studies, the biting cold that brings its own shivering misery, the indifference and the patronage one meets every day, the cold half-empty churches where one comes and goes like a ghost, the fact that I have only been invited inside two British homes since I came—one Christian, one Communist?

Am I too sensitive? Do I expect too much? Have my time-swallowing studies made me unsociable? Is it homesickness?

May I yet find Thee through the friendship and understanding of Thy people.

(f)

O God in heaven, Thou art high and lifted up, Thou sittest upon a throne, Thou art crowned with majesty and honor. No more do we think of Thee "above the clear blue sky," but in some far-flung realm of the Spirit, separated by Thy aweful glory and ethereal purity from the children of men.

So do we speak of Thee, in humble acknowledgment of Thy aloneness and otherness. But what have we done? We have used spatial terms to picture Thy bigness and holiness, and the result has been that we have convinced ourselves of Thy remoteness.

Therefore, we feel that we must search for Thee, in the heights and depths. We cry unto Thee, as though we were desperately longing that we might be heard. We turn to Thee, as the distant Last Resort. We call

upon Thee, hardly daring to hope, in our smallness and
sinfulness.

Show us what it means
to cry, Whither shall I flee from Thy Presence;
to acknowledge, God with us;
to whisper, Christ liveth in me.

10

Pattern of prayer

Adoration

Is it any use uttering words of praise when my heart
is cold?

Thanksgiving

Why are there people with many things who are
resentful and discontented, and people with few
things who overflow with gratitude; and why do I,
with a reasonable standard of living, find it so much
easier to be envious of others than to offer thanks to
Thee?

Confession

Honestly, I cannot think of anything shameful I
have done today. To make a general confession of
vague sin, and to admit that "there is no health in me"
seems artificial. And if I accept Thy forgiveness at one
moment, do I need it again the next?

Petition

Lord, if Thou knowest what is best for me before I ask, what is the point of my asking?

Intercession

Is there any use my praying for Britain, or for the sick, or for missionaries? What do I really expect to happen? How can my prayers help people far distant, or people I have never met? And if I am not asking Thee to change Thy mind about my friends, what exactly am I doing?

Meditation

Lord, my mind is full of unbidden distractions. Can I not watch with Thee five minutes?

Listening

I wait for guidance, but how can I be sure that it is Thou who speakest through my subconscious promptings, and not that other voice?

Doxology

Blessed God, help me to be conscious that it is Thee being praised, not that it is me doing the praising.

Blessing

O Lord, art Thou simply a God of general benevolence, or dost Thou act in particular ways at particular times? If indeed Thou dost act in time, in this minute rather than in that, bless me now.

33

11

Everything can be done

i

Laboratories like a physicist's dream of heaven.
Giant reactors. Charts and dials and buttons.
Power stations—the temples where men worship.
Submarines and rockets. Automation.
Sound-wave surgery and electrotherapy.
Electric razors and television.
This is my world.

A mind stimulated by absorbing work, a body decently
clothed and cared for, leisure for family and friends and
music, the undoubted necessity of a car and three good
meals a day, worship and Bible Class to lead on Sundays.
This is my life.

It is all so good. It all just happened. One thing led
to another. I am grateful, but sometimes disturbed.
Work is demanding, life is full, time is short. But sometimes, especially when I pray as I do now, I see myself
as one human unit in a total world picture crazzily different from 4 Acacia Avenue.

So many undernourished.
So many with bodies helpless against the assaults of
fever and disease, leprosy and blindness.
So many in damp, dark, overcrowded living quarters.

So many regarding the prosperous West with mingled
feelings of awe, pleading, ambition, envy, hate.
So many with fear of pain, fear of flesh, fear of spirits.

Refugees in Germany, in India, in Hong Kong. Arab
refugees, Jewish refugees. No home but a bunk fourth
from the floor. No work but to bury filth. Hope, and
no hope.
Children in Korea. Hundreds uncared for. Thousands.
This one about as tall and intelligent as my son. Need.
Crying.

None of them lives next door to me.
I sleep at night.

Babies dying. Too many mouths to feed.
Crowded islands. Unclaimed desert. Wide open spaces
guarded.
Food surplus. Famine.
Unemployment. Immigration.
Partnership, color complex, apartheid, exploitation, pa-
tronage, suspicion.
Demand for freedom, power, recognition, abundant life.
Capitalism and Communism, West and East, neutralism
and nonalignment.
Cyprus. Israel. Formosa. Germany.
Oil.

Each man in his own world, apart.
Each man seeing his own interests, over against the
interests of his neighbor.

Each man unable to see the stark alternatives of mutual life or mutual death.

I belong to a nation comparatively stable, comparatively experienced. We have won a war. I did my share.
We may no longer lead the world, but we have spirit and independence. We do not know what it is to have not.
I lack nothing. Unless it be imagination, courage, and pity.

ii

How does a Christian live in such a world?
By thinking only of the next bazaar?
By meetings, discussions, collecting boxes, retiring collections for famine relief, letters to one's representative?
By vague prayers and doing nothing?
By throwing one's scraps of money and cast-off clothing to the naked world, saying Be warmed, Be filled, Be off with you?

Married men with families and dependents cannot work in refugee camps, take economic aid to Asia, preach the Gospel of peace in Africa.
How can I help? Tithe my income? That would give support to the Church and something to spare. How be content with tithing, on my income? Old Age Pensioners tithe, and widows drop all their substance into collecting boxes.

There is nothing to spare. We need another car, to give the wife more independence. The children must be educated. The house needs another room. There is a holiday in Italy to save for.

O God, tell me, tell me once and for all, what is a Christian standard of living in such a world? Cannot the Church pronounce on this, and encourage its members to live at the Christian level? Would I follow it, if it did?

Money in large quantities could do so much. An enormous increase in government economic aid? Investment, agricultural development, industrial revolution, the sending of experts? We already feel angry at so much income tax.

Thank God a little is being done. But how little.

What more can be done?

What is God doing? How does He relieve the distressed?

Can we pray for a world like this, and leave it to perish?

What is obedience to Christ in such a world?

How can we enjoy all the good things of life with a clear conscience?

How do we face the inevitable "Inasmuch"?

How can we love our brother whom we have seen?

Surely, surely we must do something, something more, something big, something commensurate with the need and the gift of Christ?

"If enough people care, everything can be done."
Do I care enough for one?

iii

Above the roofs, out there through the study window,
I see the H-shape aerials, bringing the world's tossing
life into a box.
Above the roofs the shadow of H-for-hydrogen, threat-
ening the world's life with mushroom death.
Over wealth and poverty, over age and childhood, over
sinner and saint, tower the nuclear energies, tamed
to destroy.
Life has an X-Certificate.

Can we survive? No nation can have the bomb
in its sling, yet not be prepared to use it. Here is a
national government facing its choice—surrender of
power or principle, or all-out warfare. What then?
And here ourselves, committed by military strategy
to the use of nuclear weapons first if "necessary."
What then? Here are the nations, one by one, clamor-
ing to buy, to build, to test, to be "one of the club."
What then?

One gesture of death, provoking retaliation.
A thousand Hiroshimas at a stroke.
What horror to suffer.
What horror to inflict.

Is there something worse than a country's annihilation
in the time it takes to sweep a laboratory floor?

Dust! Man was formed of the dust of the earth, harmless dust, dust taking life upon it.

This is dust of the skies, dust more deadly than descending bombs.

Radioactive dust. Fishermen know what it brings. Argue for hours whether it causes cancer or no, argue about the nature of the deformities, argue about the burns, the sickness, the slow hand of torment. Much we do not know. What we know is too much to bear.

Mutual life or mutual death?
Can even God save us from reaping what we sow?

iv

The human race must be one, and know itself to be one.
The Gospel can make men one in Christ. Yet we do not see it conquering the world, but fighting, struggling to maintain a place. How can it challenge confident Hinduism, militant Buddhism, missionary Islam, reawakening national gods, enticing Communism, devouring materialism?
To proclaim the Gospel needs urgency, persistence, range, vision, endurance, sacrifice. A Church of God. O my soul.

To offer men God's Kingdom is worth everything.
Everything?
How much inconvenience? How much effort?
How long can the world survive without the Gospel?
What can be done now to hold a world together?

I am not a pacifist, but I ask, With man at his wits'
end, what can God use but suffering and sacrifice?
Is there a way of salvation through the utmost courage
and the utmost risk?

Where is the nation which, taking its life in its hands,
and putting its life in the hands of God, will say,
"Touch not. Handle not. We will have no truck
with this world-swallowing mouth of hell"?
Where is the nation that will say, "We have faced the
worst, and the worst is not to be armless amid the
power politics of the nations, and the worst is not
to be occupied by enemies of democracy, and the
worst is not the secret police and the detention camp
and the brainwashing, devilishly foul though these be.
The worst is to throw the universe back in the face of
God, to accept the suicide of the human race, to produce a world of the deformed, the deficient, with
monsters for great-grandchildren.
The worst is to do, not to suffer, the irrevocable deed.
Rather than that, we will die or live as slaves, if the
choice must come."

Must we view world politics as though God were
powerless?
Could God, would God, use such an act, such a
faith, such a will?
Can He bring victory, even from a bloody cross?
What other hope is there to grasp?

Nations divided within themselves. The Church divided within itself. Can the prophetic word be uttered? Can public opinion be won?

I feel so helpless.
"If enough people care, everything can be done."
Do I care enough for one,
    I a nuclear scientist,
    working in laboratories like a physicist's dream of heaven?

12

I and my Father

JOHN 10:30–38

(*a*) *"Thou, being a man, makest thyself God"* (verse 33)

O God, so many of my troubles come because I put myself where You ought to be.

I let things revolve round me—but the center belongs to You.

I like to lord it over others, even in my service, wanting to be always at the giving end, never at the receiving end—but You are the one Father of lights, the Giver of every good and perfect gift, and You seem to enjoy receiving from Your children.

I want people to respect and admire me—but my

41

light is meant to make Your face more visible to others.

I bear worry and responsibility as though I were doing it entirely alone—but only Your shoulders are broad enough to bear the sin and sadness of the world.

Now I am more than a little tired of self-centeredness and self-esteem. I am finding the business of pleasing others, and bearing their burdens, more than I can carry.

Thank God I am not God!

Save me from the blasphemy of trying to be!

(*b*) *"Say ye . . . Thou blasphemest; because I said, I am the Son of God?"* (verse 36)

Help me, O Christ, to think about Your human nature, which is also divine.

You were God-in-a-human-life, yet You were not on Your dignity.

You were Head of the human race, yet You did not boss others.

You were the Word made flesh, the Word of power and authority, yet You did not domineer or dogmatize.

You were the Magnet to whom all must come for rest, yet You were meek and lowly in heart.

God, as the prophets proclaimed Him, was always insisting that His glory and importance must be recog-

42

nized. Was that because man's deep need is to know that the Lord is great and does wondrous things, and He is God alone?

You, who existed before Abraham, emptied Yourself of all but love—was that because Your nature and Your name is love?

I see You learning and growing. I see You receiving new power and assurance at Your baptism. I see You doing many good works, the Anointed One traveling incognito, waiting for the spark of recognition and acceptance and obedience, and at last worship.

> You are He whom the Father has sanctified, whom the Father has sent.
> No man knows the Father but You. No man comes to the Father but through You.
> You alone are the Son of God. You alone can say Abba, my Father.

Yet, as the Son of God, You did not live for Your own glory, but for the glory of Him who sent You.
As man in the perfect image of God, You lived for men who had lost the image of God.
You, in whom the fullness of the Godhead dwelt bodily, identified Yourself with the fallen human race, at Your baptism of water and at Your baptism of death.

I have seen Your works in the records of Scripture, and have seen that they are the Father's works.
I have known Your works in the life of the Israel of

believers, and have glorified the Father in heaven.
I have experienced Your works in my own self-
worshiping soul, and I know and believe that the
Father is in You, and You in Him. For You, and
for You alone, it was not blasphemy to say, I am
the Son of God.

(*c*) *"Is it not written in your law, I said, Ye are gods?"*
(verse 34)

O God, is human life really formed in Your image?
Can you restore that image in everyman, defaced in
everyman by presumptuous pride?

Scripture says of the judges of old, who judged un-
justly, "Ye are gods; and all of you are children of the
most High. But ye shall die like men." Is such a high
dignity set upon man, and so low an end? Is man
capable of the glories of heaven, and liable to death?

Only one man has lived as a child of the most High.
He died like a man, but rose, and lives.
Only one man is called Son of God.
He it is who for a little while became lower than the
angels, and is crowned with glory and honor.

But He says, I and the children which God hath given
me.
He has been called the first-born of many brethren.

44

As many as received Him, to them gave He power to become the sons of God.

He says to Mary, Go to my brethren, and say unto them, I ascend unto my Father and your Father; and to my God and your God.

My Father. And your Father.

Is this the destiny of the children of men?

Are we constantly setting too low a value on human life?

Are we indeed to be sons of the living God?

Does this mean me?

> Am I supposed to share in the divine Nature?
>
> Am I to receive the Spirit that made Christ what He was?
>
> Can Your peace, Your very joy, be mine?
>
> Am I to live as a cell of the Body of Your only Son?
>
> Have I received the spirit of adoption, whereby we cry, Abba, Father?

Then why should I not walk with head held high, forgiven and free?

Why should I not face the future with confident hope, careless of what may come?

Why should I not meet all my daily concerns with the exciting consciousness that I am an heir of all the wealth of Your Kingdom?

Why should I not live always in the light of the promise,

> All things are yours,
>
> > and ye are Christ's,
> >
> > > and Christ is God's?

45

Then shall I walk and not faint.

Then shall I draw near with boldness to the throne of the heavenly grace.

Then shall I speak to You with loosened tongue, as a son to his Father.

Is any among you afflicted? let him pray. Is any merry? let him sing psalms.

Is any sick among you? let him call for the elders of the church; and let them pray over him, anointing him with oil in the name of the Lord:

And the prayer of faith shall save the sick, and the Lord shall raise him up; and if he have committed sins, they shall be forgiven him.

Confess your faults one to another, and pray one for another, that ye may be healed.

JAMES 5:13–16

13
Bowed in prayer

The lamp burns over the curtained ark where the books of the Law are kept. It has been like that since I first came here, a lively young girl. Soon the books will be brought out for the readings. It is a strain to look up sideways toward the lamp. Better to keep staring at the floor's rough patterns, and the feet of my neighbors. Better to close my eyes in prayer, only then I catch myself praying the prayer of the years, that the crooked be made straight. Better not to pray; better to submit. There has been plenty of time to learn submission. Best of all, to forget myself in the solemn praise of God. The Benedictions:

"With great love hast Thou loved us, O Lord our God; with great and overflowing pity hast Thou pitied us! O our Father, our King, for our fathers' sake, who trusted in Thee, and whom Thou didst teach the statutes of life, be gracious unto us, too, and teach us. . . . A God that worketh salvation art Thou. . . . Blessed art Thou, O Lord, Who choosest Thy people Israel in love!"

Yes, Israel is loved by God. In all the years of my anguish, I have never doubted that. Was not Israel helpless and nameless, till God took him and gave him His Law? Then does He not pity each and every member of His people? Does His salvation reach even the smallest and humblest, reach even a woman? Am I not a daughter of Abraham? Then my voice must not be silent as the Shema is recited:

"Hear, O Israel: the Lord our God is one Lord: and Thou shalt love the Lord thy God with all thy heart, and with all thy soul, and with all thy might. . . .

"Take heed to yourselves, that your heart be not deceived, and ye turn aside, and serve other gods, and worship them. . . .

"I am the Lord your God."

Blessed be God! We stand in silence while the prayers are said. My neighbor's hand supports my elbow. She is a good woman. Bless her, Lord. It is my brother's voice I hear in prayer. This is not the

first time the ruler of the synagogue has chosen him
to pray in front of the ark. He praises the name of
God. He prays for the afflicted, and holds me in his
heart. He thanks God for the visitor who moves
among us, one who by God's power heals the sick and
casts out demons. We join in the Amen.

"Blessed art Thou, O God, Giver of the law."

Now the book comes out, and the congregation is
hushed. Lord, I love Thy Word. There are seven
men to read the Law today, for it is the sabbath. Verse
by verse, I wait for the sacred Hebrew to be trans-
lated into the language I speak.

*"The Lord did not set His love upon you, nor choose
you, because ye were more in number than any people;
for ye were the fewest of all people:"*

Why then should God so care for us through the
generations, even to the promise of the final consola-
tion of Israel?

*"But because the Lord loved you . . . hath the Lord
brought you out with a mighty hand, and redeemed you
out of the house of bondmen."*

O my Lord, is there redemption still from the
house of bondmen? The book is rolled up, and the
readers have gone to their places. Now the familiar
psalm:

"I will extol Thee, my God, O King; and I will bless Thy name for ever and ever. Every day will I bless Thee. . . ."

Every day I have tried to bless Him. It is easiest when we are here together. Life is sweeter for praise. God is good to let us praise Him. Let me think of that, as the singing goes on.

"The Lord upholdeth all that fall, and raiseth up all those that be bowed down. . . ."

Can this be Thy word to me, O Lord, who am so bowed in body and spirit? . . . Now will come the reading from the Prophets. There is an unusual excitement in the air. I can feel it around me. It is agony to try to raise myself to see. My neighbor whispers that the ruler has called upon the visitor to read. Much was being said of him before the service began, some of it with admiration, some of it with anger. They say he is against the Law and the priests. Then why does he worship in our synagogue? They say he speaks of the Kingdom, and performs many signs of the Kingdom. Then why is the face of the ruler so white and tight? One glimpse of him, at the cost of pain, is enough. He does not welcome his guest, who now takes the book.

"The spirit of the Lord God is upon me. . . ."

His voice is soft and strong. He radiates authority. His feet are all I can see of him, but they speak good news of peace.

"He hath sent me . . . to proclaim the opening of prison to them that are bound. . . ."

Them that are bound! There are more prisoners than those behind walls. Is it God who binds his children, giving a measure of life to those He has hemmed in? Can there ever be deliverance for the bound? Why is my heart thumping and my breath difficult? Do not be a fool, woman. Nothing is changed. Year in, year out, it has been the same. The synagogue service is as it always is. Except for the visitor.

The reading is over. The book is closed and put away, under the lamp. Now he speaks. He speaks of the freedom which belongs to the children of the Kingdom. I listen. . . .

The final benedictions!

"Blessed art Thou, O Lord our God, King of the universe, Who openest the eyes of the blind.

"Blessed art Thou, O Lord our God, King of the universe, Who clothest the naked.

"Blessed art Thou, O Lord our God, King of the universe, Who loosest them that are . . ."

Them that are bound! I knew those words would

come again. I was waiting for them. I was terrified lest this once they should be left out. They came!

Is our God He who unties knots? Is not this the work of the Messiah when he comes? Will he not be the strong Deliverer, the giver of joy and liberty? How beautiful upon the mountains are the feet . . . the feet . . . of him that . . .

Can this be he? How wonderfully he spoke! They say he forgives sins, cleanses lepers, casts out demons. They say he blasphemes by claiming the prerogatives of God. "The Lord our God is one Lord." "Take heed to yourselves, that your heart be not deceived." God is one God! How can a man be divine? The sacred blessings are upon God alone.

The Service is complete. People are already moving. More than ever, in spite of all my attempts to be calm and sensible, there is a bewildering, persistent expectancy in me, a vibrating song that makes the heart thud upon the ribs, and the locked bones tingle.

The visitor is there. He looks at me. Only his feet and legs are in my vision, but I know he looks at me. I am held by his look. Now he comes nearer, nearer. I see his hands. They are lifted toward me. He calls. Calls me. Me to him. It is the sabbath day. Ought not a daughter of Abraham to be loosed from her bond on the sabbath day?

I come, Lord. I, a woman bowed down with a spirit of infirmity for eighteen years, come.

.   .   .   .

"Blessed art Thou, gloriously blessed, O Lord our God, King of the universe, who by Thy prophet Jesus of Nazareth raisest up them that are bowed down."

LUKE 13:10–17

14
Midnight meditation

Almighty God, I have asked Thy help these many times, but it does not come quickly. So often I am depressed and in despair, and I am ashamed to think how easily the tears flow. Since my wife died, I have discovered that I am an old man, with little to light my path. They have been good to me here. Best of all have been the times when I have made a friend of a fellow voluntary patient, and we have walked the green lanes together. But they come and go. I have nothing to go to. I hate to walk alone.

I have been a Churchman all my life, and in my humble way have tried to live up to it. I have been kind and meek by nature, and glad to be so. Now this thing has swept me off my feet, has turned me in upon myself, has gone over my head like a flood, and left me without heart and without hope. I cry to Thee. Canst Thou hear my feeble and desperate moan?

We must count our blessings. There is much beauty and quiet in this place. But often my eyes look at the blossom with no delight. Sometimes visitors come. They

53

cannot know how much their casual conversation lifts me into a new world of light.

I have not been to Church here. That was because I felt I could not stand it, not because I have lost my belief in Thee. I am afraid to feel deeply, lest my sorrow swallows me up.

This afternoon the chaplain came. We do not see him often. He has far too many to visit. He came today, and he could see I wanted to talk. We stood in the hall of the villa, away from the noise of the radio and the TV, and he talked of Thee.

He didn't invite me to the Sunday Service, and he didn't tell me to pray more, and he didn't tell me I needed more guts (as a clergyman did once), and he didn't tell me to snap out of myself. In a way, he disappointed me. I did not get what I expected and thought I needed. He told me to think about Jesus Christ, and to see Thee in Him. He told me Thou art a God of health and peace, and that Thou art all the time busy to make men whole.

He told me to turn my thoughts away from these weighty burdens toward Thee. He told me to sit for minutes together, as relaxed as I possibly could be, saying over and over, "I am the Lord who loveth and healeth thee." He said that Thou canst not work without faith, and that faith is not making a desperate effort to believe something, but turning to Thee in mind and heart again and again.

So I have been trying, and now—lying in bed—this is the longest prayer I've prayed since I was admitted.

54

My mind keeps coming back to myself, and how things have worked out, and how I had to come to this place, and how alone I am, and how little the future has for me. If only we'd had children. If only I'd been more patient with my wife in those last years. If only she were still with me at home.

I'm doing it again! "I am the Lord who loveth and healeth thee."

15
A walk home

i

Cancer of the intestine. It is almost a relief to be sure. It is something to have an hour to walk, and possibly pray, before Susan expects me home from work. There is quite a bit of sorting out to do. Pray. What am I supposed to pray? "Thy will be done, and that's the end of it." That takes some praying. I am not sure that I can manage it. Ought I to manage it? It sounds Christian enough, but . . . . The Muslim would pray it. Muslims are devout. I saw them at their prayers in Egypt. Submission—that is the meaning of the word "Islam." Allah knows best, blessed be the name of Allah. This is the Lord's doing, and it is ghastly in our eyes. It is the Lord: let Him do what seemeth Him good, however bad it seemeth to us. I am not made of that kind of stuff.

ii

What alternative is there? Curse God and die. But perhaps I shall not die for months or years. It must be a wearisome business cursing God for so long. To use a phrase, there doesn't seem much future in it! I thought I knew something about God, enough to love Him a bit. Nothing is clear any more.

iii

Tom with his Christian Science would say, and *will* say (what a variety of friends I have to face), it is all a mistake. Pain isn't real! Suffering is an invention of the mind—mortal mind I think he calls it. Why in God's name should any sort of mind want to think up anything as awful as this? It's against all common sense. I shall know pain is real enough before it has finished with me. Nobody wants to suffer, least of all a man with a good job and children and a wife who is all that a wife should be. I've heard Susan call Christian Science utter nonsense. Anyway, it sounds like the wanderings of someone who is less Christian than most and no scientist at all. Tom can't help me.

iv

Who can help me? The doctors. Of course, they will do what they can. People recover from cancer these days —some people. He made it pretty clear that he would have had a better chance if I'd gone to him sooner. How could I know what had got me? Be frank, I said. Tell me the worst. It was worse than the worst I'd dreamed of. We need more research, he said. There isn't enough money. How much money makes an H-bomb? We'll do all we can, he said. His eyes said, It isn't much we can do. . . . They can't help me.

v

Who can, then? God, can You help me? Why have You sent this? What have I done to deserve it? Are You punishing me? What have I done? I heard a Jehovah's Witness say on the doorstep once that all suffering is divine punishment for sin. That might be true enough of some suffering in some circumstances. But it isn't VD I've got. The pagans think that disease is caused by the anger of a god. At the first twinge of toothache, they hurry off to the priest to get on the right side of the gods again. (Toothache. There's some sense in *that* kind of pain the red light, warning you that something must be done. But the pain that eats your body away, the pain that can only be drugged and endured, endured to breaking point, what is the sense in that?) Didn't the Jews believe that suffering was vengeance from heaven? Each man shall suffer for his own sin! Cheerful news!

vi

What did Jesus think about that? Rabbi, who did sin, this man or his parents? What was the answer? Neither! Neither! And then something about the works of God being made manifest. Well, they were. The blind man

saw again. Is that a clue? The Gospels are full of heal-
ings. But it doesn't seem to happen any more. There
are faith healers, and I have heard of some parsons laying
their hands on people. It always struck me as a bit odd,
even though it seems to work sometimes. I've heard our
minister talk of the Church's ministry of healing. What
does that mean? Mission hospitals in Labrador? What
else?

vii

The Church does not seem to believe in God's power
to heal any more. Sermons on suffering are all about
discipline. Suffering tests us. Suffering shows what we
are made of. That Lenten fellowship meeting—didn't
we learn that "trial" is the same word as "temptation"
in the New Testament? Strange to think of it now, but
I looked up that passage in I Peter. The trials his readers
were suffering seem to have been persecution for the
faith. At least, one can understand *that* kind of agony.
There's point and purpose in it, just as there was in the
Cross. I should like to think I've the guts to be a martyr
under State persecution, or to go as a missionary to a
fever-infested area. But this thing I've got makes nonsense of everything. Is it really God testing my faith and
improving my character?

viii

Job! He wasn't punished for his sin, in spite of all the
assertions of his comforters. His faith was being tested.

And it was Eli who said, It is the Lord. . . . Perhaps he could. I can't. I suppose these coming months could make me a better man—more patient, more submissive, more . . . Christian. Is that what I have to pray for, Lord? Heaven knows (and probably hell) how easy it is going to be to turn into a person who is moody, depressed, short-tempered, weak, resentful, and unbelieving. Is suffering an endurance test? Then why do doctors spend all their time trying to get rid of it? Why do we all accept without question the idea that it is better to be well than ill? The Church seems to approve of all efforts to heal. Why, if God sends disease for our good? Is it after we have tried all possible remedies without success that we ought to say, "God is putting me through it to make a better man of me"? If that were so, the more medical science advances, the less God decides that men need discipline! When did Jesus ever say, "Endure it, my dear fellow, and see God's love in it"? He might have done so, but He didn't. Why not?

ix

Jesus healed men, and we believe He was God's perfect Word. O God, can it be that I misjudge You? Have we all painted Your character too black? Have we been afraid to believe in Your utter goodness and love, and to act upon it? "In Him is no darkness at all." So many men have sunk into doubt when suffering came. Is that because, in the hour of crisis, the Church could only mutter "mystery," "judgment," "discipline," as the sum of its Good News? We cannot love a God who is less concerned to make His children happy than a human father is. We cannot believe in a God who is nothing more than a Pious Policeman, only concerned to see that men keep the Law and get punished if they don't. The Father of Christ was not like that. You are not like that.

x

Then what do You really want for our human species? Your will is the Kingdom our Lord said He came to bring! Heaven on earth! The end of uncleanness, and of "sorrow and sighing"! The restoring of the universe to perfection! If the Bible is true, nothing less than that can be Your purpose. Then does it mean that at the beating heart of the universe there is a will, effectively willing good for the children of men? Salvation is health, and health is harmony, and harmony is wholeness, and wholeness is holiness, and You offer all this to men in Jesus Christ. Can that be true? All He ever did and said cries out that it is.

xi

Then why pain and suffering, disease (that's dis-ease!) and death? That is too much for me. A lot of illness seems to be caused by sheer ignorance, ignorance of how to defeat harmful bacteria (some have been defeated), and ignorance of how human beings ought to live (and we are constantly finding out more). But why should men be ignorant of what promotes their true welfare?

How much are we responsible for our ignorance, or for not acting and planning according to our knowledge?

xii

The Bible speaks of a fall. It shows that a lot of suffering is the result of man's misuse of the powers You gave him. It speaks of the travail of a new world coming to birth. It says that this is the sort of world where Your will is often not done. There is a contradiction at the center of things. You have made a creature with a will of his own. How it is possible for Your will not to be done is beyond our understanding. We have to face it as a fact.

xiii

There is also quite a lot in the New Testament about principalities and powers. Are these part of the furniture of minds unenlightened by modern scientific discovery? Or is there more in it than that? My educated West African friends are still very conscious of evil forces. Are these forces deep in the mind, or do they exist outside us? I seem to remember that some modern psychologists are not prepared to dismiss altogether the idea of demon possession.

xiv

What it all adds up to is this: there is a kingdom of darkness as well as a kingdom of light! The darkness may consist of human ignorance, human carelessness and rebellion, deep destructive forces in the depth of the human personality, and—it may be—other rebellious wills in Your universe which have a profound influence on man. However we think of it, the darkness is real enough. Have we had the courage to face the reality of this darkness? Have we tried to soft-pedal the discord of the universe? Have we, in doing so, muddled in our thinking the kingdom of light and the kingdom of darkness, painting the world of experience, and getting our colors mixed? In minimizing the black side of things, have we even given You a bad name? Have we been so concerned to call You omnipotent, that we have not dared to face the Biblical truth that, although all things are in Your hands and allowed by You, You are only omnipotent *in the end?* (That is some comfort.)

xv

Then can we see illness as Jesus saw it, as a manifestation of the kingdom of darkness? "This woman whom *Satan* hath bound eighteen years" . . . "a messenger of Satan to buffet me" . . . "If I by the finger of God cast out demons, then is the Kingdom of God come upon you." Like us, Jesus thought that disease was the very devil!

xvi

Why have I never seen it before? Why doesn't the Church make it plain? If this is the sober truth, then You are fighting suffering with the same intensity with which You fight sin! You are against it! What a relief it is to know that! But what does it mean? Surely it means that Church leaders are right who practice the laying on of hands and anointing with oil. These things are not to be left to strange sects. They are Your command, Your gift, to Your Body the Church. It means that prayer can be offered for the sick, with faith and expectant trust, knowing that we are not trying to overcome a grudging reluctance, but accepting the invitation to be fellow workers with our God. It means that all Your divine energies are toward healing, and that doctors and psychologists and ministers and the whole Body of believers are Your instruments. It means that I can pray and ask others to pray that I may be healed!

xvii

Suppose I'm not! Does that mean I am back where I started? No. No. I can still be entirely consecrated to You, who are all light and love, and utterly worthy to be loved. I see that there are many barriers to healing— our lack of faith, the atmosphere of unbelief in which we live, our ignorance of the spiritual laws which the Lord used in meeting each man's particular need, the doubts and fears and resentments of the subconscious mind beyond our direct control, hostile powers, it may be, outside man. Let me look constantly at Christ, for increase of faith. Let me worship, and make thankful use of all the means of grace and healing in the Church, and so live in an atmosphere of faith and hope and love. Let me seek to know more of the things that make for health and peace. Let me meditate constantly upon the simple and glorious affirmations of the faith, so training the subconscious in truth and serenity. Let me pray no more with reservations and anxieties, but in the childlike acceptance of Your perfect ways.

xviii

Let me, in sickness and in health, in life and in death, say—not with resentful submission, but as the most positive desire of my heart, "Thy will be done."

Our street at last.

Help me to share it all with Susan.

16

The tongue of the dumb

(*a*)

You are not here, Jesus of Nazareth. So I shall just have to pretend you are. You do not know it, but I have been your faithful disciple for three days, ever since I heard the story of how you healed the little Greek girl. You said to me, "Reuben, follow me. I can do with a boy of ten to help me with my work." I said I would.

Now I want to talk to you about my Father, because the villagers say you will be passing along this road to-day, and they are going to bring my Father to you.

I should like to bring him myself, but they say I am

too young and not important enough. They say the village elders are the right people to approach a prophet like you.

There are hundreds of people here already, sitting about in groups and watching the road. All we have seen so far are three Roman soldiers and a couple of mangy camels. They have not come with Father yet. He will hate all these crowds. I like crowds, Jesus, but not today. Today I hate them, with Father. I am keeping away from them.

You see, Jesus, he is not like other men. He is big and strong and good, but he is different from all the others. He has never heard my voice. They say he has not heard his own voice since the day it was high-pitched like Mother's and mine. I suppose that is why he gets nowhere when he tries to talk. What comes out is just a sort of mumbling. I think I know what he says better than Sister or Mother or anyone. But it is not the words that tell me. They get lost in a babble like a foreign language.

My poor Father. They push him around so when he wants to be quiet. Only my Mother and I understand him. You would understand him, Jesus. He loves the Lord God, and he is clever with his hands. But he cannot join in the gossiping and grumbling of the others. He stands apart, and they despise him. Can you understand that?

This morning they wrote on a writing tablet, "We are taking you to see the prophet." I think he knew something of what they meant, but he looked alarmed.

He cannot bear to meet strangers. You are a stranger to him, Jesus. You are a stranger to me, too, but it is good to pretend we are friends.

There is Father now, surrounded by the village men. There is no place for me there. He will not see me with this crowd between us. He looks lost and sad. The crowd is thickening.

What are you going to do, Jesus of Nazareth, when you come this way? I can never be your follower again if you will not help us. I can never speak to you again.

Now the crowd in the distance is stirring. Are you really coming? Is that you with your older followers? The people are jostling and shoving, but they are making way. Our villagers are hurrying toward you, Father in the middle of them. What will you do?

You have greeted them courteously. You seem to have told them to wait, for you are bringing Father away with you, away from the crowds he hates. You are leaving the crowd and coming in this direction. How glad I am to be here! Father is too busy looking at you to notice me.

I can see everything you do. You say nothing. What use would that be? Father has been in the quiet of the grave for longer than my life.

You sigh, and look upward to heaven. Father is watching you.

You are putting your fingers into his useless ears. Father is feeling you.

You are spitting on your finger, and touching his tongue. Father is tasting you.

EPHPHATHA. *Be opened*. Your voice is like a trumpet sound, rousing the dead.

What has happened? Does Father hear you? He stands with the strangest look on his face I have ever seen. Jesus, Jesus, can he hear you speak to him? His lips are moving. Is it the old mumbling, or does he speak to you plainly? Can he hear himself speak? Will he be able to speak to me?

The crowds are running and shouting, and here am I running faster and shouting louder than any of them. Father, my Father, can you really hear me? Did you speak my name?

Father, hold me, hold me tight. I did not mean to cry.

Jesus, Master, I am your disciple. You did it. You have done all things well. You even make the deaf hear, and the dumb speak. Father and I thank you.

MARK 7:31–37

(b)

Lord, for long years I have been deaf and dumb.

I always knew that there were men who heard a voice
    that I never heard.
I always knew that there were men who spoke a lan-
    guage that I could not understand.
I think as a child I had ears and a mouth, but time dimmed the spiritual senses.

For years, the language of grace has been a foreign language.

For years, I have been a stranger to the voice of prayer. I could only mutter.

Since Thou didst come into my life, my ears have been opened. The voice of the woods is a new voice, and the sound of my child's laughter is a new sound, and the songs of Zion are new songs.

I have found Christ in mouth of friend and stranger.
Thy Word in Scripture has become a lively Word.
Thou hast called me by name, and spoken to my heart,
    and I have recognized Thy voice.
    Once I was deaf. Now I hear.

With Thy Spirit within me, my words come without stammering. The dumb they are talking of Jesus's grace.

I would speak boldly, as I ought to speak.
I would learn the language of love.
I would praise Thee with the voice of mirth and thanks-
    giving.
I would pray with unsealed lips.
    Once I was dumb. Now, in Thy Presence, I speak plainly.

POSTBACK

(in explanation of the subtitle of the book)
The infant Christian
1. is the "natural man" converted;
2. has been born into a new world;
3. is a stammerer;
4. is learning to talk.

I

The infant Christian is the "natural man" converted

(a) *the meaning of conversion*

The subtitle offers this book to the "infant Christian." Who is he? In the preface it is suggested that he is the "natural man" after conversion. But what is that?

The word "conversion" is a clannish word. Perhaps it always was. In certain circles it is used without apology, and without ceasing. Elsewhere, it is one of the Samaritans with whom the Jews have no dealings. It is a fact that the word seldom occurs in our English Bible, and when it does, it has little of the emotional and intellectual clothing in which it has often been draped.

The simple meaning of "to convert" is "to turn," whether to turn a farmhouse into flats, or like the bells, to make Sir Richard Whittington "turn again." Its Biblical meaning is to turn to God. The New Testament

Greek word is "epistrephein," which translates the Hebrew word "shub" and other Hebrew words. Two verses
indicate its meaning, and the infant grammarians will
note that it is used transitively in the first, and intran-
sitively in the second:

"And many of the children of Israel shall he turn
to the Lord their God." (Luke 1:16)

"And all that dwelt at Lydda and Saron saw him,
and turned to the Lord." (Acts 9:35)

The Revised Version nearly always keeps to the literal
translation "turn again"; the Authorized Version does
sometimes use the word "convert." Read Mark 4:12,
Matthew 18:3, Luke 22:32, Acts 3:19, James 5:19, and
then take a deep breath. You will see that it is not possible to read into the word as it occurs in these passages
the later theological, technical definitions. The actual
noun "conversion" occurs only in Acts 15:3, where Paul
and Barnabas pass through Samaria, "declaring the conversion of the Gentiles," which means that the Gentiles
have "turned" to God, by placing their faith in Jesus
Christ who has been preached to them.

(b) *conversion and repentance*

This half-day excursion into the dales of Biblical scholar-
ship (and we shall see later how often this is needed)
shows how near "convert" is to "repent," which means
"re-turn to God." The repentant "convert" faces an-

other way. Before, he had turned his back on God. Now he looks in the face of God, and lives. Any sort of turning may be swift or slow, gradual or sudden, but this need not blind us to the fact which every hiker knows, that there is a difference between facing south and north.

Turning to God, with repentance and faith (that word needs defining too) can happen in all kinds of ways. The essential thing is that God's activity is behind it. God converts. Even the act of repentance can only happen by grace. However active a man may be, however much or little stirred in his emotions, he is, at the moment of faith, the passive recipient of a new life and a new look:

> "I rose with joy to relate to my parents what God had done for my soul, and declared to them the miracle of God's unbounded grace."
>
> (Testimony of Henry Alline in William James's *Varieties of Religious Experience*)

"What God had done"—that is the language of the converted.

(c) *turning points*

Many of the difficulties about the word "convert" arise because different people use it of different stages in the Christian experience. We may say of a World Series ball player that his career started when his mother attended sandlot matches in what *Good Housekeeping* would call "a dress for the waiting time," or when at the age of ten months he delivered a curved pitch from his baby carriage, or when he played in the back garden or had his first coaching at school, or when he hit a home run in his first game for his college.

Each of these was a "turning point." His attention was caught in a new way. His look in the direction of "America" was restored, renewed, and intensified. It was baseball that did it.

We may refer here to the two-cents' worth of concentrated profundity in *The Way of Integration* by Professor H. A. Hodges of the University of Reading. Professor Hodges, writing of the growth of the personality toward integration, summarizes the stages of growth as they have been defined in traditional Catholic ascetic theology. There is the "purgative way," the stage when a man believes in God, but is more conscious of His law than of His active grace; the "illuminative way" which brings a personal relationship with Christ, and deeper insight into spiritual realities; and the "unitive way" when every vestige of the "old man" has gone, and the soul is fully committed to God.

In a fascinating comparison between this classification and Methodist evangelical teaching, he asserts,

> " 'Conversion' in Methodist language means the transition from the purgative way into the illuminative."

Then he adds,

"Immediately after his conversion, Wesley went about puzzling his friends by saying that he had never been a Christian until then. That is as much to say that the purgative way is no part of the Christian life. This was certainly a mistake. The conversion experience is truly a new beginning in the spiritual life, but it is not the first beginning of that life altogether, and I think much damage has sometimes resulted from thinking that it is. Wesley himself later withdrew from this position, and expressed the view that before his conversion he had had a genuine faith, but the faith only of a servant, and that afterwards he had the faith of a son." (pp. 36, 37)

The fact is, however, that all our classifications must confess their inadequacy before living experience. As for the question with which we started long ago, as to what was meant by the conversion of the natural man, we may say this: when the natural man turns to God, through faith in Christ, he has made a beginning, and the beginning is a true beginning, and the beginning is only the beginning.

2

The infant Christian has been born into a new world

(*a*) *another world*

Our Lord's way of describing the new beginning through faith is by comparison with the birth of a child:

"You must be born again." When the Holy Spirit breathes His life, the experience is like emerging from the darkness of the womb into a light and freedom which bring release to all our latent powers.

John Wesley has described this transition in delightful detail in his sermon on "The Great Privilege of Those that are Born of God." He says of the infant,

> "His ears are unclosed, and sounds rush in with endless diversity."

The spiritual senses are opened to a new and exciting environment, which is God. Wesley says that the coming of the Spirit effects

> "a change in the whole manner of our existence; for, from the moment we are born of God, we live in quite another manner than we did before; we are, as it were, in another world."

Another world! Notice especially that when men enter another world, they need to learn a new language. We have not yet reached the point in our educational program when it becomes necessary to include the language of Mars as a subject. We English have enough trouble with the speech of those who live twenty miles away across the channel. But a new world means a new speech. Every "realm" of human experience has its own medium of expression, and a new experience needs a new vocabulary to express that experience. We have only to think of the worlds of chess and cricket, philosophy and flying, to see the truth of this.

The Church is a "new nation," a holy people (I Peter 2:9, 10), and like every other tribe on earth, has its own language.

(b) *a new vocabulary*

Thus it is that every child born into the world must soon begin language study. And every infant Christian has a new vocabulary to learn.

We have already been at pains to define the Christian word "convert." Many other terms have a specialized Christian meaning and use which each generation has to learn afresh. They often need meticulous redefinition, and in our time many Biblical theologians have set out to bring a new truth and vitality into the terminology of the new world of the Spirit. Dr. William Barclay's *A New Testament Wordbook* is a recent example.

These Christian words constantly need guarding against backsliding. They will wander away like lost sheep, given half a chance. They repeatedly need converting. Thus "grace" needs a new precision of outline; "faith" must throw off both its colorful and its shoddy trappings, and stand before us naked and unashamed; "hope" demands a stiffer backbone; and "love" needs rescuing from the corruptions of lust. "Salvation" must go under the linguistic microscope; "justification" must be ferreted from hiding; "redemption" must lose its shame of the pawnbrokers and the prisoner-of-war camp; and "holiness" must be firmly led from the stained-glass window to the decisions of the businessman.

Some may make a bold attempt to do without this theological shorthand altogether, like a child who is slow in learning to speak because it knows it can get what it wants by grunting! What needs to be remembered is that these words all stand for deep truths of God's dealings with men. They were invented to describe experience of the new life. They come to us with a challenge to the heart, as well as to the mind. They come bearing ageless promises. What matters is that we are living in the new world, and finding the reality its language expresses. The Church needs its "interpreters," who will try to convey what is meant to "those outside," but no infant Christian should neglect his language study. (See Prayer 8.)

(c) a new tongue

There is more in a language than nouns. So the infant Christian has more to learn than the great doctrinal names. He must learn something about pronouns—the "I-Thou relationship" about which so much has been written. He must ponder the depths and heights of the all-significant preposition "in," for his life is now "in Christ." He must see to it that his character merits the right adjectives! He must face the fact that the main part of speech for every Christian is the verb, and especially the verbs "to be" and "to do." He must realize the importance of the adverb, for there is surely a distinctively Christian way of doing the simplest things. He must live out his life in conjunction with others.

In this way he will seek to communicate with those whose ears are not yet "unclosed," and also with his fellows in Zion's city. He will learn the language of the heart, the grammar of grace, the syntax of sanctification, and the style of love. Above all, he will learn how to speak to his Father. Can he manage that? What language is sufficient to offer praise and thanksgiving to the eternal God? How inadequate language is to express the invisible motions of the spirit. And how terrible if when the language is carefully chosen, it expresses something that is not there at all, and the beautiful liturgy becomes but vain repetition. How much the infant Christian has to learn! (See Prayer 10.)

3
The infant Christian is a stammerer

(a) backward children

The epistle to the Hebrews chides those who ought to be older brothers, taking responsibility in the family, but who instead need to be taught all over again the "ABC" of the oracles of God. Such is the literal meaning of "first principles" (Authorized Version) in Hebrews 5:12. Why is it that infant Christians take so long to grow up?

It is when we try to pray that the need for sanctification of personality, and the maturing of judgment, are seen most clearly of all. Then is revealed, in private to ourselves when we catch our own eye, and in public to others, our underlying attitude to our Creator, and our grasp of the language of the Spirit. How often we pray with "stammering tongues"! (See Prayer 1.)

Wesley describes the attempt of the man upon whom "God comes unawares" to turn to prayer:

"He begins . . . to pray to Him; although, through fear and shame, he scarce knows what to say. But whether he can speak or no, he cannot but pray, were it only in 'groans which cannot be uttered.' "
(Sermon on "The Means of Grace")

This is the earnest attempt of the man who is still in the "purgative way." The pity is that, perhaps through our own self-neglect, we stay so long amid its disciplines and stammerings.

(b) a foreign language

What is the cause of our "stammering" in prayer? Two clues are given us—one ancient, one modern. In the Old Testament, the most frequent use of the word "stammer" is in reference to speech in a foreign language.

In Isaiah 28:7–13, the drunken priests and prophets mock Isaiah, saying that when he speaks to them he treats them like children, giving his message in a silly baby talk. They parody his message as "tzaw latzaw tzaw latzaw, kaw lakaw kaw lakaw," literally meaning "commandment on commandment . . . , rule on rule. . . ." Stammering jargon! Isaiah takes up this

78

taunt, saying that God will indeed speak to them in a strange, foreign tongue. When the Assyrian invaders are talking to one another in their hearing, that will be God speaking to them!

In a later passage, the people are told that in the glorious time coming Jerusalem will no longer be besieged by the foreign armies, those "of a stammering tongue, that thou canst not understand" (Isaiah 33:17–24).

Isaiah's language sounded to the citizens of Jerusalem like the stammerings of a foreign tongue because their ears were not attuned to the Word of God. It was they who could talk fluently—with the fluency of strong drink. But their godless conversation was really the stammerings of men for whom the divine oracles were as strange as the speech of Assyria.

In the same way, much will sound strange to the infant Christian. He has to learn the language of the new world he has entered as though it were a foreign tongue. He must not expect to be able to speak it naturally. How will he overcome his stammering? He must learn the new language as every child does, by placing himself constantly where it is spoken. If he neglects the Word of God, and "the assembling of yourselves together," he will remain a stammerer. But as he lives in the new environment, he will discover that what at first sounded like a foreign tongue is actually the language of the homeland. (See Prayers 5 and 8.)

The exciting thing about this growing up is that the Father Himself constantly addresses us as though we understood. C. S. Lewis somewhere uses this simple fact to explain the meaning of justification. God insists upon treating us as though we were already His innocent children, though He knows very well we are not so innocent! God insists upon dealing with us as though we could already share His deep thoughts like full-grown men, though He knows very well we cannot! But how could any infant learn to talk, unless people spoke to him as though he already knew the language?

(c) nervous causes of stammering
Secondly, the modern clue to our stammering is in the writings of speech trainers and child psychologists, who among other things are concerned with defects in speech. For example, Dr. Benjamin Spock in his popular *Baby and Child Care* writes,

> "We know that a child's emotional state has a lot to do with stuttering. Most cases occur in somewhat tense children. Some stutter only . . . when talking to one particular person. . . . Stuttering may start when a father decides to be stricter in his discipline."

Does the infant Christian stutter because he is not yet completely at home in his Father's house? Does he bring with him into the new life some of the fears and worries and guilt feelings of that old world of God-less self-sufficiency? Has he yet to learn to relax in the glorious assurance of God's pardon and peace? Is he more conscious of the laws of the household than of the

Father's infinite purposes of good for all His creatures? Does he grow more tense than ever when the circumstances of life seem to indicate a tighter discipline? Is God the "one particular Person" before whom his voice falters? Has he yet to find at the foot of the Cross the secret of security? (See Prayers 13–15.)

Dr. Spock tells us that stuttering often occurs when a naturally left-handed child is made to change to right-handed. The doctrines of creation and original sin may be expressed in exactly those terms. We were born to hear God and to speak to Him, but the demanding claims of sin have forced us into an unnatural way of self-centered living. (This, of course, is using the word "natural" in a way different from that in the phrase "the natural man.") No wonder we are tense! Christ's invitation is to a balanced emotional state, in which the heart and the words flow smoothly. (See Prayer 12.)

4
The infant Christian is learning to talk
(a) plenty to say

It is as we begin to live with the Father in the family, and find our peace in His presence, that we shall grow more talkative. When children gain confidence, what a flood of words comes out!

One of the marks of the Messianic age was that the tongue of the stammerer should speak plainly. (See the Epilogue.) No doubt one reason why the disciples recognized Jesus as the Messiah was that in His presence, that is what happened. On the day of Pentecost, the apostles found a new loosening of the tongue, and they spoke "as the Spirit gave them utterance" (Acts 2:4). The Christians who took part in the free, spontaneous worship of the earliest days were very young in the faith, but they had plenty to say. Paul's problem was the problem of all teachers in the presence of eager children—to see that they spoke one at a time (I Corinthians 14:26–33).

The liturgy of the Church grew up out of the desire that all things be done decently and in order. Perhaps the healthy Church is the one that values liturgical beauty and order while at the same time cherishing and encouraging the gift of extempore prayer. In the *Didache,* probably written early in the second century, we find a form of service for Holy Communion, with the comment added,

"But suffer the prophets to give thanks as much as they will."

(b) *speaking freely*

This freedom is further stressed by the widespread use of the word "parresia" in the New Testament. It was used in classical Greek of the democratic right of the citizen of Athens to speak his mind in the public assembly. So in Grimm-Thayer's Lexicon it is defined as "freedom in speaking," "unreservedness in speaking."

The last verse in the *Acts* tells us that Paul was able to speak in Rome with "parresia." (See Prayer 7.)

So the word comes to mean "free and fearless confidence," "cheerful courage," and I John 4:17 insists that this is the attitude of the justified Christian before God on the day of judgment! It also describes the present attitude of the Christian in his prayers:

> "Seeing then that we have a great high priest . . .
> let us therefore come *boldly* unto the throne of grace."
> (HEBREWS 4:14–16)

The Christian can talk to God freely, and without reserve, in the confidence of a loved child. (See Prayers 3 and 4.)

This freedom, let us notice, is the result, not of education, in its broadest or narrowest sense, but of faith. We have all met unlearned men who in prayer rose to sublime heights of devotion and expression, speaking as only men who are inspired speak. The Spirit prays within them and through them.

In the terminology quoted by Professor Hodges, this ability to speak before God belongs to those whose feet have been well set upon the "illuminative way." Speaking of their private prayer, he writes,

> "With the mind's eye fixed steadily upon some one of the mysteries of God, the heart plays around it a symphony of acts of faith, hope, love, penitence, adoration, thanksgiving, and the like; and this 'af-

fective prayer' now supplements and partly replaces the habit of praying in set sentences. Prayer comes to consist less and less of saying things in words, more and more in looking quietly at God and worshipping."

(*Ibid.*, p. 33)

When one has learned the language, there is less need to use it! (See Prayer 14.)

Professor Hodges goes on to say that as the soul progresses on this path, it meets darkness and dryness. He says this aspect of growth has been much neglected in the thinking of Protestants.

"The soul is tempted to think she is deserted and going backwards. But she is not. She is being purged of all delight in prayer in order that she may learn to pray not for the sake of . . . delight, but of God alone. She is being taught the lesson which so many refuse to learn, that the core of religion is not 'religious experience' but simply a quiet naked adherence to God for His own sake. The soul passing through this 'dark night' is quite safe, provided that the loss of pleasure in prayer does not quench her desire to pray."   (*Ibid.*, pp. 33, 34)

Amid periods of dryness, the soul must on no account "dry up." (See Prayer 9.)

(c) *"I spake as a child"*
There are, of course, the further heights of contemplation, but the infant Christian must be prepared to take

the next step. Perhaps he is sometimes discouraged by his slow progress. Perhaps he feels that he is indeed an infant

"with no language but a cry."

Perhaps he sees all the stages of growth and sanctification before him, and sees himself as a mere stammerer. (See Prayer 16.)

But let him not think of himself as a "mere" anything. He is a sinner saved by grace! He is an adopted child of God! Let him not be ashamed of his stammerings. A child of the Kingdom does not mind speaking in short syllables. He must go on talking, and listening. John Wesley likens this process to the breathing of the new infant:

"The same breath which comes from, returns to God: as it is continually received by faith, so it is continually rendered back by love, by prayer, and praise, and thanksgiving; love and praise and prayer being the breath of every soul which is truly born of God. And by this new kind of spiritual respiration, spiritual life is not only sustained, but increased day by day, together with spiritual strength, and motion, and sensation, all the senses of the soul being now awake." ("The Privilege of Those that are Born of God")

Let not the infant Christian stop breathing for a moment! (See Prayer 2.)

The prayers in this book have been written to encourage the man who speaks as a child to go on speaking, to be himself in the holy Presence of God, to turn his thoughts (however inadequate) into prayers (however faltering), to live more and more in the real freedom of the children of God. (See Prayers 6 and 11.)

Our encouragement is that no infant can possibly remain an infant so long as he continues to breathe! Growth may seem slow, but if we are alive in Christ, we cannot help growing in Christ. The Yorubas of Nigeria have a proverb which sums up our longing and our certainty:

"However much the child may stammer, he will learn to say 'Father' in the end."

QUESTIONS FOR GROUPS

(Some help with the answers will be found in the "Notes" that follow, but the main purpose has been to arouse thought, stimulate discussion, and promote action. The Group may like to list points where further help is required, and as a last desperate resort, to call in the minister.)

1. Under correction (pp. 1–3)

Take the quotations one by one, and see if you can state

    (*a*) the situation in which the words were spoken;

    (*b*) why the question or statement needed correction;

    (*c*) how Jesus answered it.

Then turn up the passage, as given in the "Notes."

2. For all occasions (pp. 3–9)

    (*a*) What does it mean to you that Christ will be "all in all" at the end of history?

    (*b*) Well, how? What help is available?

    (*c*) Please advise the lady.

    (*d*) Examine the pledge in the Covenant Service. What hinders our complete dedication?

    (*e*) What is spiritual power, and how is it to be grasped?

    (*f*) Any suggestions?

(*g*)　What does the cross mean to you so far?

(*h*)　What is the best way of celebrating the Resurrection? How can we experience the Resurrection?

(*i*)　How important are our feelings?

(*j*)　What is the meaning of each of these pictures? They are all Biblical. See the "Notes."

(*k*)　What are the effects of the coming of the Holy Spirit?

(*l*)　What is the value of the doctrine of the Trinity to us? On what is it founded?

(*m*)　Is the Gospel demand or offer?

(*n*)　What is your idea of the ideal Sunday School Anniversary?

(*o*)　Do we over- or under-emphasize the thought of God as Creator?

(*p*)　"Missions disturb settled and happy tribal life." "We need all our money and energies to evangelize at home." How would you answer these two objections?

(*q*)　"I'm not good enough to stay to Holy Communion." How would you answer that comment?

(*r*)　Is this your experience? What conclusions do you draw from it?

(*s*)　What is the value of confession to another? Should it always be to a priest or minister?

(*t*)　Some people grow tired and weary in their service. Must this happen? How is it avoided?

(*u*)　Why is it important for a Christian not to be dull?

(*v*) Does God's forgiveness mean that we need not bother too much about sin?

(*w*) What is the Christian attitude to the rest of living things?

(*x*) What is the place of sport in the Christian life?

(*y*) "I left the world of business because I could not be a Christian in it." Comment.

(*z*) What is the Christian way of going to bed?

3. *Weather—or not* (pp. 9–10)

Do you ever pray for fine (or wet) weather? Why or why not?

4. *Let your yea be yea* (pp. 10–12)

What is the attitude of a man praying "the prayer of faith"?

5. *The great congregation* (pp. 13–16)

(*a*) In what frame of mind should we listen to a sermon?

(*b*) What are your views on the furnishings of our churches?

(*c*) Should we go to, or stay away from, worship according to who is preaching?

(*d*) Would a louder and readier response from the congregation make our worship more alive? Should the congregation take more part in worship than they usually do in Free Church worship?

(*e*)   What things in us make our relationships with other people difficult?

(*f*)   What are we supposed to be doing when the organist is playing the voluntary?

(*g*)   What are your views about children's addresses?

(*h*)   How important is it to have helpful and beautiful things to look at in Church?

(*i*)   Do you want the story simply? If it is simple and you know it already, why do you want to be told?

(*j*)   Why do people avoid the front seats if they possibly can? Can and should anything be done about it?

(*k*)   Do you always think of what you are singing about? Why not? What can be done about it?

(*l*)   Why do you come to Church?

(*m*)   Why is there a reluctance to accept responsibility in Church life, and elsewhere?

(*n*)   In our worship and prayer, how should we deal with distractions, including human ones?

(*o*)   How would you tackle this whole problem of new and old tunes?

6. *Visible Church* (pp. 16–19)

What is the *minimum* requirement for a man to be a Christian?

What is the *minimum* requirement for a Church to be a "true" Church?

What is meant by the phrase "a true Church"?

7. *A mouth and wisdom* (pp. 19–23)

(*a*) Which prophets are speaking in these three quotations?

(*b*) How would you answer a person who said "Politics is too dirty a game for a Christian"?

(*c*) Why do you think there is a shortage of trained teachers of religious knowledge? What can be done?

(*d*) What help can be gained by using prayers from a book?

(*e*) Who from?

(*f*) In the matter of sex education, what do you think are the responsibilities of (*a*) parents, (*b*) teachers, (*c*) the Church?

(*g*) How is embarrassment to be avoided when a person is speaking in public? Is such embarrassment sufficient reason for *not* speaking in public?

(*h*) How would you decide whether you had a call to the Ministry? How would you be certain that God was *not* calling you to the Ministry?

8. *Praying with the Bible* (pp. 23–28)

You   What does it mean that our life is "hid with Christ in God"?

Sheep   Should a Christian be receiving training with others? What sort of training should be available?

Send forth In what ways are we perhaps too wrapped up in ourselves?

Wolves	What sort of difficulties do we experience as Christians living among non-Christians, and what do we do about them?
Wise	Where do we need to apply this "practical wisdom"?
Harmless	What is involved in obeying the command, "Judge not"?
Behold, I	How do we know that God has chosen us?

A general question—Is this a method of prayer and meditation which we might practice? See "Notes" for suggested texts to start with.

9. *Very dry* (pp. 29–32)

(*a*) Should we pray when we don't feel like it? Should we pray when God seems remote?
(*b*) What is the answer to this sense of need?
(*c*) How does a Christian "refuel in flight"?
(*d*) How can we have a deep assurance of forgiveness and restoration?
(*e*) How can we help overseas students in this country?
(*f*) Do we sufficiently stress the transcendence of God? Do we sufficiently stress the immanence of God? What results from neglect to do either?

10. *Pattern of prayer* (pp. 32–33)

Adoration: Is it?
Thanksgiving: Why?

NOTES AND
BIBLICAL REFERENCES

(All the passages in the text are from the Authorized Version—except No. 8 from the Revised—but that is to save time and trouble and the infringement of copyright. The reader is advised to use modern translations on every possible occasion, and in retirement—or before, if possible—to make his own.)

Preface

The following are a few among many helpful books:

About prayer
Denis Lant, *First Steps in Prayer*, Carey Press.
Bernard Clements, *When Ye Pray*, SCM Press.
David N. Francis, *About Prayer*, Epworth Press.
Olive Wyon, *The School of Prayer*, Westminster Press.
Evelyn Underhill, *Abba*, Longmans.

Prayers for private use
Wesley's Hymns.
John Baillie, *A Diary of Private Prayer*, Scribner's Sons.
E. Milner-White, *My God My Glory*, S.P.C.K.

Liturgical prayers, for private and public use
The Book of Common Prayer.

Methodist Book of Offices.
Divine Worship.
George Appleton (ed.), *In His Name,* St. Martin's
    Press.
Nathaniel Micklem, *Prayers and Praises,* Independent
    Press.

Inquire of the Lord

John 16:23. See note under this verse in William Temple, *Readings in St. John's Gospel.*

1. Under correction

(*a*) Luke 12:13. Reply verses 14–21.
    John 6:28. Reply verse 29. Note the change from
        "do" to "believe."
    Mark 9:22. Reply verse 23, especially in Revised
        Version, or Revised Standard Version.
    John 4:11–12. Reply verses 13, 14, 26.
    John 3:4. Reply verses 5–8.
    Matt. 11:3. Reply verses 4–6.
    Matt. 8:21. Reply verse 22. The meaning of the
        disciple's words is probably, "I'll be glad to fol-
        low you, after my old dad is dead."
(*b*) Mark 8:4. Reply verses 5–9.
    John 9:2. Reply verse 3.
    Luke 17:5. Reply verse 6. Their faith does not need
        to increase; it needs to be alive.
    Mark 13:4. Reply verse 32.
    Acts 1:6. Reply verses 7, 8.
(*c*) Luke 5:8. Reply verse 10.
    Matt. 17:4. Reply verses 5, 8. Moses the giver of

the Law, Elias = Elijah, representative of the prophets. Peter puts Jesus on the same level as the greatest men of the past dispensation. That is not high enough!

Matt. 18:21. Reply verses 22–35.

Mark 14:29. Reply verse 30.

Luke 22:33. Reply verses 31, 32.

John 13:37. Reply verse 38, and chapter 21:15–19.

John 21:21. Reply verse 22.

(*d*) Luke 10:40. Reply verses 41, 42.

John 6:9. Reply verses 10–14.

John 14:5. Reply verse 6.

John 14:8. Reply verse 9.

2. *For all occasions*

(*a*) Compare the message to the Churches from the Assembly of the World Council of Churches, meeting in Evanston, 1948: "We do not know what is coming, but we know who is coming."

(*b*) See Collect for 2nd Sunday in Advent.

(*d*) See Covenant Service from the Methodist Book of Offices.

(*j*) Acts 1:9–11; Mark 16:19; Acts 7:55; Rev. 3:21.

(*n*) Songs of Praise 557.

(*x*) Ps. 121:8.

3. *Weather—or not*

Ps. 77:18; Ps. 29:10; Ps. 19:4–5; Matt. 8:27; 1 Kings 17:1; James 5:17.

4. *Let your yea be yea*

The title is from James 5:2, quoting our Lord's words
  recorded in Matt. 5:37.

Matt. 7:7; Mark 11:23–24; 2 Cor. 1:19, 20 (see
  Phillips' translation); Luke 11:13; John 16:23, 24;
  Matt. 7:11.

Compare Charles Wesley, *Methodist Hymn-Book*
  (M.H.B.), 510:

> "If what I wish is good
> And suits the will divine;
> By earth and hell in vain withstood,
> I know it shall be mine."

5. *The great congregation*

(*a*) M.H.B. 390, verse 3.
(*b*) Ps. 1:1.
(*c*) I am indebted to Mr. W. C. Jarvis for this authen-
  tic prayer.
(*f*) Matt. 6:3; Ps. 18:36.
(*h*) Heb. 11:27; 2 Chron. 20:21.
(*i*) M.H.B. 161.
(*j*) 1 Samuel 3:1–10.
(*k*) M.H.B.
(*m*) Ps: 84:10.
(*o*) M.H.B. 6, verse 3.

6. *Visible Church*

Matt. 18:20; 1 Cor. 12:12–31; Charles Wesley,
  M.H.B. 761; Jer. 14:9.

The reader may object that these are the thoughts, not the prayers, of a man. But what is prayer but thinking and desiring in God's Presence?

7. *A mouth and wisdom*

(*a*) Moses—Ex. 4:10. Reply verses 11, 12.
Isaiah—Is. 6:5. Reply verses 6–9.
Jeremiah—Jer. 1:6. Reply verses 7–10.
Compare Solomon—1 Kings 3:7–10.

(*g*) The answer on this occasion was, Anything you like so long as you don't put them in your pockets.

8. *Praying with the Bible*

You	Matt. 10:2; Mark 3:14; "you"—e.g., Luke 22:28; Col. 3:3.
Sheep	"flock," e.g., Ezekiel 34; John 10:16; John 10:4.
Send forth	M.H.B. 457.
Wolves	Isaiah 53:7, compare 1 Peter 2:21–25.
Wise	1 Cor. 1:25; Luke 16:8; James 3:17; Gal. 6:10.
Harmless	2 Cor. 11:3; 1 Cor. 13:5.
Behold, I	"called" Rom. 8:30; John 10:14, 15.

A few suggestions of verses from this chapter which might be treated in a similar way are verses 7 and 8, verses 19 and 20, verse 22, verses 34–37, verses 38 and 39. But any verse in the Bible may be used!

9. *Very dry*

The title is taken from Ezekiel 37:2.

(*a*) Rev. Dr. R. Newton Flew advises the use of this prayer in "dry" seasons.

(*b*) See the Postback for some possible answers to this question.

(*f*) Isaiah 6:1; Heb. 2:9; Deut. 30:11–14; Rom. 10: 6–9; Ps. 139:7; Matt. 1:23; Gal. 2:20.

10. *Pattern of prayer*

Petition: Matt. 6:8.

Intercession: James 5:15, 16.

Meditation: Mark 14:37.

11. *Everything can be done*

The quotation, "If enough people care, everything can be done," is from the closing words of Victor Gollancz, "The Devil's Repertoire," a very moving study of "nuclear bombing and the life of man."

12. *I and my Father*

The whole passage John 10:30–38 needs careful study.

(*a*) 1 John 5:21.

James 1:17; Matt. 5:16; 1 Peter 5:7; John 5:44.

(*b*) Phil. 2:6, 7.

John 1:14; Matt. 11:28–30.

Ezekiel 12:15, 16; Ps. 86:10; John 8:58; M.H.B. 371, 339.

Matt. 3:16, 17; Acts 10:38; Matt. 28:17.

John 10:36; Luke 10:21, 22; Mark 14:36.

John 8:50; M.H.B. 842, verse 6; Col. 2:9; Matt.
   3:15; Luke 12:50.

Matt. 5:16; John 10:38.

(c) Gen. 1:27; Rom. 8:29.

Ps. 82.

Heb. 2:9.

Heb. 2:13; Rom. 8:29; John 1:12; John 20:17.

Hosea 1:10; 1 John 3:1; 2 Peter 1:4; Rom. 8:11;
   John 14:27; John 15:11; 1 Cor. 12:27; Rom.
   8:15.

John 8:36; Rom. 8:21; Rom. 8:17; 1 Cor. 3:21–23.

Isaiah 40:31; Heb. 4:14–16; Luke 1:64.

13. Bowed in prayer

There is some doubt about the exact form of the synagogue service at the time of our Lord. The only con-
temporary references are in the Gospels, especially Luke
4:16–28, but no doubt the later account in the "Mishna"
can be followed closely. Details are given in Evelyn
Underhill, *Worship,* esp. pp. 208–213. See also Dix,
The Shape of the Liturgy, pp. 37, 39. A delightful list
of Jewish blessings is in Gollancz, *A Year of Grace,*
pp. 60–64.

The Benediction quoted is the Second Benediction
before the Shema, given in Oesterley, *The Jewish Background of the Christian Liturgy.*

The Shema consisted of Deut. 6:4–9, Deut. 11:13–

21, and Numbers 15:37–41. The word "Shema" is the first Hebrew word—"Hear."

The "Law" which was read consisted of the first five books of the Old Testament. The particular passage quoted here is Deut. 7:7–8.

The Psalm sung is Ps. 145. It "was more frequently sung than any other and it was believed that whoever recited it three times in the day would attain eternal life." Underhill, *op. cit.*, p. 216.

The passage from the Prophets is Isaiah 61:1–3. It was quoted by our Lord in the synagogue at Nazareth (Luke 4:18), and it seems very likely that He would read it on other occasions.

"A sermon or lecture followed the reading of the Scriptures and this could be given by anyone competent so to do. The preacher sat during his discourse." *A Standard Bible Dictionary*, p. 835.

Medically speaking, the suggestion has been made that the woman was suffering from a hysterical paraplegia. Weatherhead, *Psychology, Religion and Healing*, p. 60.

14. Midnight meditation

For a very brief account of the value and practice of meditation, see *Some Thoughts and Prayers for Your Healing*, published by the Guild of Health, Edward Wilson House, 26 Queen Anne St., Harley St., London W.1.

For a fuller account see M. V. Dunlop, *Introduction to Contemplative Meditation*.

15. A walk home

   i. Matt. 26:39; Ps. 118:23.
  ii. Job 2:9.
   v. Deut. 24:16.
  vi. John 9:2, 3.
 vii. 1 Peter 1:6, 7.
viii. Job 1:6–12; 1 Sam. 3:18.
  ix. John 1:14; 1 John 1:5.
   x. Matt. 6:10; Luke 12:32.
 xii. Gen. 3:17–19; Rom. 8:22; Isaiah 1:2; Acts 17:30.
xiii. Eph. 2:2, 6:12.
xiv. Rev. 11:15.
 xv. Luke 13:16; 2 Cor. 12:7; Luke 11:20.
xvi. Mark 3:15; Mark 16:18; James 5:14, 15.
For further reading:

    L. D. Weatherhead, *Psychology, Religion and Healing* (pp. 62 ff., 97 ff., for demon possession).

    J. Wilson, *Healing through the Power of Christ.*

    Report of Archbishop's Commission on "The Church's Ministry of Healing."

16. The tongue of the dumb

The title is from Isaiah 35:6.

(*a*) The man was "kophos" (here = "deaf") and "mogilalos," which literally means "speaking with difficulty." This last word sometimes translates the Hebrew "dumb." Another word for dumb is in verse 37. The words in verse 35 support the view that the man "had an impediment in his speech" (Authorized Version,

103

Revised Version, Revised Standard Version), i.e., he "stammered" (Moffatt). An alternative reading of the Greek word gives "hoarse of speech." Either way, he was not dumb, but "had not even heard his own voice for a long time, and so speaks in a muttering way hard to follow" (Weatherhead). Weatherhead says that the bound tongue was thought to be caused by the spell of a special demon. He emphasizes how Jesus made contact with the man through all his available senses.

See V. Taylor, *The Gospel According to St. Mark.*
L. D. Weatherhead, *Psychology, Religion and Healing,* p. 69.
(*b*) See John 10:4; Eph. 6:20.
M.H.B. 392, verse 5; 329, verse 3.

Postback

The books quoted and mentioned are:
The Holy Bible.
William James, *Varieties of Religious Experience,* Modern Library.
H. A. Hodges, *The Way of Integration,* Epworth Press.
John Wesley, *Forty-four Sermons,* Epworth Press.
William Barclay, *A New Testament Wordbook,* Harper & Brothers.
C. S. Lewis, *Beyond Personality,* Macmillan (especially Chapter 7).
Benjamin Spock, *Baby and Child Care,* Duell, Sloan and Pearce.

EPILOGUE

ISAIAH 32:1–4; LUKE 11:2; ROMANS 8:26, 27;
ROMANS 8:15; LUKE 1:64; PSALM 51:15.

Behold, a King shall reign in righteousness, and princes shall rule in judgment.

And a man shall be as an hiding place from the wind, and a covert from the tempest; as rivers of water in a dry place, as the shadow of a great rock in a weary land.

And the eyes of them that see shall not be dim, and the ears of them that hear shall hearken.

The heart also of the rash shall understand knowledge, and the tongue of the stammerers shall be ready to speak plainly.

When ye pray, say, Our Father.

Likewise the Spirit also helpeth our infirmities: for we know not what we should pray for as we ought: but the Spirit itself maketh intercession for us with groanings which cannot be uttered.

And he that searcheth the hearts knoweth what is the mind of the Spirit, because he maketh intercession for the saints according to the will of God.

For ye have not received the spirit of bondage again to fear;

but ye have received the Spirit of adoption,
    whereby we cry,
        Abba, Father.

And his mouth was opened immediately, and his tongue
loosed, and he spake, and praised God.

O LORD, OPEN THOU MY LIPS;

AND MY MOUTH SHALL SHEW

FORTH THY PRAISE